ESL FOR BEGINNERS:
Lessons Guide with Activities
VOLUME ONE

A Comprehensive Guide for Teaching English to Child/Adult Speakers of Other Languages

D1332258

www.bilinguallearner.com

This book is dedicated to the students and English-speaking staff of ADPP Escola de Profesores de Futuro in Chimoio, Mozambique....I am so grateful for your graciousness in welcoming me into the EPF family- your hospitality and friendship made *ESL for Beginners* possible.

Like and follow Bilingual Learner on Facebook and Twitter to see our weekly posts on developments in the ESL/counseling world and to receive our newest free/low cost products!
www.bilinguallearner.com
www.facebook.com/bilinguallearn
www.twitter.com/bilinguallearn

For information on this publication or others by this author, visit the website or contact the author at the email address below.
Special discounts are available on quantity orders.
www.bilinguallearner.com
bilinguallearner@hotmail.com

RECOMMENDATIONS FOR TEACHING *ESL for BEGINNERS*

Back in 2007, when I was living in Bolivia, I noticed a mysterious phenomenon at my American-International school where I worked as an ESL resource teacher. Every year, like clockwork, about 2-3 students per homeroom would start sifting out from the rest of the class in December - these were the kids who just couldn't pick up English as fast as the rest of the group. For a multitude of reasons, these struggling kiddos would try and try and just not seem to grasp their second language. These strugglers were my students. They were an amazing, playful, hopeful challenge for me and I was a home base for them- where they could relax a little and slow down, learn English at their own pace and feel little less self-conscious about their language struggles. I also spent some time teaching English to adults in Africa and used many of the same activities as with my elementary students- obviously tweaked a bit to fit the different cultures and age groups. And I also use some of these activities on a weekly basis now in the Texas public school system with the students I work with who are "Newcomers" to the USA. Here are the practices that work best with all my different groups of students:

- Included in this guide are sixteen beginner level one lessons. They can be taught over any time span, but for the fastest English acquisition, I recommend meeting with students Monday-Thursday for about 2-3 hours to teach these lessons at the pace of 1 lesson per day. Be sure to give a 10 minute break per hour. If you follow this schedule, the lessons guide should take about one month to complete. If you would like to continue to use this series to teach your ESL students, you can find *ESL for Beginners- Volume II* at the website **www.bilinguallearner.com**.
- As noted above, each lesson can be lengthened or shortened because many of the activities naturally allow for this. For example, you can sing all the songs or play multiple games in one lesson to lengthen the lesson time to three hours. Conversely, you can split a dialogue presentation over two days, with half the class presenting the first day and the other half presenting the second day in order to shorten the lesson to one hour.
- While these lessons are appropriate for ages six to adult, you might simplify some of the written activities so very young students can repeat/copy your example, rather than read on their own.
- Start your class with an assessment (Appendix B) so you have a baseline of where students are when they start with you; if you give the same assessment at the end of Volume One, you can determine how much progress has been made and where else they need support.
- For ESL classes in a general education school setting, set up your ESL resource group of students by asking for teacher referrals of the students who struggle the most with speaking/understanding English in their classrooms. Once you have a list of students to work with, send home the parent notification letter (Appendix A) and assess each student (Appendix B) for grouping and data purposes.
- I usually divide students into groups by the English Speaking Levels (beginning, intermediate, advanced) listed in Appendix B. Occasionally, I run two different groups for the BES students (beginners) if there are students who have never spoken/heard English AND students who have a basic English foundation.
- I've found that the best way to communicate with students is to speak clearly, slowly, repeat everything twice, and throw in just the tiniest bit of native language only when absolutely necessary.

RECOMMENDATIONS FOR TEACHING *ESL for BEGINNERS* (continued)

- When working on speaking chorally with students (ex: with numbers/alphabet review cards), here are the steps I follow:
  1. I pronounce the letter/sound/sentence while they listen only.
  2. I pronounce it again and students repeat.
  3. We pronounce it together.
  4. They pronounce it as a group without me.
- Each day I start off the lesson referring to chart paper or the chalk/whiteboard where I've written the day of the week, the date with month/day/year, and a list of our day's activities. Here's how I introduce this:
  1. I read and they listen to the pronunciation.
  2. We read it together.
  3. A student translates it so all understand the day's activities.
- All of my lessons include Circle Time- this is perfectly appropriate for the little ones all the way up to adults. I have small children sit on the floor in a circle around me; older children and adults sit around me in chairs.
- When having students read aloud, I like to work in a Round Robin fashion- meaning that each student reads a portion aloud as we come to them moving in a circular clockwise fashion. I explain at the beginning of every lesson that anyone who doesn't want to read aloud can just say "pass."
- I give prizes to the big kids and adults too. In all my years working with kids and adults alike, I've never had anyone turn down a prize.
- This lessons guide combines excellently with the culture group sessions guides, *ESL for Beginners Culture Explorers* OR *ESL Survival Skills*. With these cultural guide, you can lead your students on an exploration of the traditions and lifestyle of a country in the western world. You can find this guide and other products at the website: **www.bilinguallearner.com.**

ESL FOR BEGINNERS- Volume One
Focus: Speaking and Understanding Oral Language

THEME ONE- SCHOOL

*Objectives: The student will:
- Practice greeting and saying goodbye
- Practice saying the letters of the alphabet
- Practice saying the numbers 1-10
- Speak about *School* and understand *School* vocabulary
- Use the *To Be* verb forms in a dialogue, chant, and spoken/written sentences
- Listen to and understand a short story

*Materials
- Appendices C-I and L, chart paper, index cards, prizes, markers

*Activities
- Start each lesson with Circle Time where the teacher greets each student, the class reads the day's date/activities together in English, and a student translates so all can understand the lesson's activities. Then, do the *School* vocabulary card warmup (Appendix C) and do the alphabet/1-10 number card reviews (Appendix D) with students.
- Each day there is a different main activity to learn or practice the English theme for that week. Below are the 4 main activities, one for each day plus a starred extra activity that you can divide between the four days if you'd like to extend your daily lesson.
  1. *To Be* Chant (Appendix F)
  2. To Be Structure (Appendix L)
  3. *To Be* Dialogue (Appendix E)
  4. Short Story #1 (Appendix G)
  *Extra Activity- Greetings Dialogue (Appendix E)
- Finally, meet back in a circle for the Circle Speaking Activity (Appendix H).
- It's always motivating to end each lesson on a fun note with a 10 minute game where students can win a prize. See Appendix I for a list/description of games.
- Say goodbye to each student individually and they respond.

THEME TWO- HOME

*Objectives: The student will:
- Practice greeting and saying goodbye
- Practice saying the letters of the alphabet and spell out their name orally
- Practice saying the numbers 11-20
- Speak about the *Home* and understand *Home* vocabulary
- Use the verb *Can* in sentences
- Express not understanding with common phrases
- Orally answer short story comprehension questions

*Materials
- Appendices C-I and L, chart paper, index cards, prizes, markers, scrap paper

*Activities
- Start each lesson with Circle Time where the teacher greets each student, the class reads the day's date/activities together in English, and a student translates so all can understand the lesson's activities. Then, do the *Home* and *School* vocabulary card warmup (Appendix C) and do the alphabet/11-20 number card reviews (Appendix D) with students.
- Each day there is a different main activity to learn or practice the English theme for that week. Below are the 4 main activities, one for each day plus a starred extra activity that you can divide between the four days if you'd like to extend your daily lesson.
  1. *Alphabet Song* (Appendix F)
  2. *Spell Your Name* (Appendix H)
  3. Can structure (Appendix L)
  4. Short Story #2 (Appendix G)
  *Extra Activity- Common Phrases: write each of the following phrases on chart paper and follow the same 3 steps as you do for introducing the day's activities, then give each student a chance to say the phrases in response to a statement they don't understand.
  -I do not know.
  -I do not understand.
  -I cannot.
- Finally, meet back in a circle for the Circle Speaking Activity (Appendix H).
- End each lesson on a fun note with a 10 minute game where students can win a prize. See Appendix I for a list/description of games.
- Say goodbye to each student individually and they respond.

THEME THREE- NATURE

*Objectives: The student will:
- Practice greeting and saying goodbye
- Practice saying the letters of the alphabet
- Review pronunciation/meaning of numbers to 1-20
- Speak about *Nature* and understand *Nature* vocabulary
- Sing/speak about nature we observe in our environment
- Understand the difference between demonstrative words: *this, that, these*, and *those*

*Materials
- Appendices C-I and L, chart paper, index cards, prizes, markers

*Activities
- Start each lesson with Circle Time where the teacher greets each student, the class reads the day's date/activities together in English, and a student translates so all can understand the lesson's activities. Then, do the *Nature, Home,* and *School* vocabulary card warmup (Appendix C) and do the alphabet/1-20 number card reviews (Appendix D) with students.
- Each day there is a different main activity to learn or practice the English theme for that week. Below are the 4 main activities, one for each day plus a starred extra activity that you can divide between the four days if you'd like to extend your daily lesson an extra 30 minutes to 1 hour.
  1. Demonstratives Structure (Appendix L)
  2. *This and That* song (Appendix F)
  3. *Can I ...?* dialogue (Appendix E)
  4. Short Story #3 (Appendix G)
  *Extra Activity- Demonstratives Dialogue (Appendix E)
- Finally, meet back in a circle for the Circle Speaking Activity (Appendix H).
- End each lesson on a fun note with a 10 minute game where students can win a prize. See Appendix I for a list/description of games.
- Say goodbye to each student individually and they respond.

THEME FOUR- PERSONAL HYGIENE

*Objectives: The student will:
- Practice greeting and saying goodbye
- Practice saying the letters of the alphabet
- Practice speaking about numbers and birthdays in a dialogue
- Speak about *Personal Hygiene* and understand *Personal Hygiene* vocabulary
- Sing a song about personal hygiene
- practice using verbs in the present tense
- Orally answer short story comprehension questions
- Review pronunciation/meaning of numbers to 1-20

*Materials
- Appendices C-I and L, chart paper, index cards, prizes, markers

*Activities
- Start each lesson with Circle Time where the teacher greets each student, the class reads the day's date/activities together in English, and a student translates so all can understand the lesson's activities. Then, do the *Nature, Personal Hygiene, Home,* and *School* vocabulary card warmup (Appendix C) and do the alphabet/1-20 number card reviews (Appendix D) with students.
- Each day there is a different main activity to learn or practice the English theme for that week. Below are the 4 main activities, one for each day plus a starred extra activity that you can divide between the four days if you'd like to extend your daily lesson an extra 30 minutes to 1 hour.
  1. Present Tense Structure (Appendix L)
  2. *This is the Way* song (Appendix F)
  3. *Numbers/Birthday* Dialogue (Appendix E)
  4. Short Story #4 (Appendix G)
  *Extra Activity- Observation Walk (Appendix H) or LEA activity (Appendix H)
- Finally, meet back in a circle for the Circle Speaking Activity (Appendix H).
- End each lesson on a fun note with a 10 minute game where students can win a prize. See Appendix I for a list/description of games.
- Say goodbye to each student individually and they respond.

*If you are continuing on with *ESL for Beginners- Volume Two*, you can find it and other products at www.bilinguallearner.com.

PARENT NOTIFICATION LETTER

August, 2012

Dear Parent,

Your child, _____, has been selected work 4 days a week in a small group to improve her/his English speaking and understanding.   While your child is making progress in communicating in the English language, we would like to take this opportunity to give him/her some extra English language support.   These classes will meet Monday through Thursday for 1 hour in Ms./Mr. _____'s classroom.   It is very important that your child attend each class.   If you have any questions, please call me at school.   Thank you very much for your support.

Sincerely,

_____

Teacher

_____

SPANISH VERSION

Agosto, 2012

Querido Padre,

Su niño/a, _____, ha sido seleccionado para trabajar 4 días a la semana en un pequeño grupo para mejorar su Inglés oral y comprensión.   Mientras su niño/a esta progresando de una manera consistente en la comunicación del lenguaje Inglés, nos gustaría darle esta oportunidad a su niño/a con un apoyo extra en Inglés.   Estas clases serán Lunes hasta Jueves por una hora en la sala de Señora/Señor _____.   Es muy importante que su niño/a atienda a cada clase.   Muchas gracias por su apoyo.   Si tiene preguntas, por favor llámeme a la escuela.

Sinceramente,

_____

Maestra/o

ESL Diagnostic Test

Name _____

Primary Language_____

Grade _____

Birthday _____

Date _____

Student's ESL Level _____ (TO BE ASSIGNED AFTER ASSESSMENT)

Directions: Complete the following assessment with each student in your group right before you start the Theme One lessons. Administer this assessment individually to each student by sitting in a quiet place with them and asking them each question/prompt below in English. You will need to use the picture below and a box of 12 crayons for some of the questions/prompts. Write down their answer and move to the next question/prompt. After the student has finished a level of the assessment, have them do a quiet activity near you while you score the level by making a tally in the correct/incorrect column using the attached Scoring Key. After you've made all the tallies, count them and reference the attached Scoring Guide for that level to determine if you should administer the next level of the assessment. Also, use the Scoring Guide for each level to find the student's ESL level and write it on the correct line above. Give this same assessment again after the Theme Four lessons to see what progress the student has made and to determine further areas of focus for the student.

www.bilinguallearner.com

Beginning English Speaking (BES) Level Scoring Guide- Direct the student to complete all the following questions/prompts by answering you in English after you read them the prompt in English. If the student scores 3 or more errors, stop at this level because the student is at the Beginning English Speaking (BES) Level and mark BES level on the front page. Alternately, if the student scores 2 or less errors, continue onto the Intermediate Level of the assessment.

CORRECT/INCORRECT

1. What is your name? _____ ____   ____

2. Where are you from? _____ ____   ____

3. What letter does your name start with? _____ ____   ____

4. How old are you? _____ ____   ____

(Put a 12 box of crayons on the desk for the next 3 questions/prompts)
5. How many crayons are in the box? _____ ____   ____

6. Put a crayon on your paper. ____   ____

7. Can you draw a road with the crayon? _____ ____   ____

(Show attached picture for next 5 questions)
8. *(point to girl)* What is this? _____ ____   ____

9. *(point to sun)* What is this? Tell me in a sentence.
_____ ____   ____

10. This is a tree. There are 6 _____ ____   ____

11. *(point to boys)* In this picture, what are they doing?
Tell me in a sentence. _____ ____   ____

12. In this picture, the girls are sitting and resting. They have been playing sports all day before they took this picture. Now they just want to rest. Do they feel angry or tired now?
_____ ____   ____

End of Level. Score answers to know if student should proceed to next level.

www.bilinguallearner.com

Intermediate English Speaking (IES) Level Scoring Guide- _Direct the student to complete all the following questions/prompts by answering you in English after you read them the prompt in English. If the student scores 3-7 errors, stop at this level because the student is at the Intermediate English Speaking (IES) Level and mark IES level on the front page. If the student scores more than 7 errors, stop at this level, but rate them as BES-high and mark this on the front page. Alternately, if the student scores 2 or less errors, continue onto the Advanced Level of the assessment._

CORRECT/INCORRECT

(Show attached picture again for next 3 questions)

1. What is at the top of the picture? _____ ___ ___

2. How many arms and legs are in the picture, total? __ ___ ___

3. What do you think the boys in the picture did yesterday? Tell me in a sentence.
_____ ___ ___

4. What did you eat yesterday? Tell me in a sentence.
_____ ___ ___

5. Tell me how you spell your name. _____ ___ ___

6. When is your birthday? _____ ___ ___

7. Tell me some good things about your family in a sentence.
_____ ___ ___

(For the next 2 prompts, ask student to repeat the following sentences after you- say each only once.)

8. I like to eat bananas. _____ ___ ___

9. The girl is named Sue and the boy is named John.
_____ ___ ___

End of Level. Score answers to know if student should proceed to next level.

Advanced English Speaking (AES) Level Scoring Guide - _Direct the student to complete all the following questions/prompts by answering you in English after you read them the prompt in English. If the student scores 2 or less errors, the student is at the Advanced English Speaking Level and mark AES on the front page. If they score more than 2 errors, the student is still at the Intermediate English Speaking Level and mark IES on the front page._

CORRECT/INCORRECT

(Show attached picture again for the next 4 questions below.)
1. Tell me 3 things you think might happen in this picture.
_____
_____
_____   ____   ____

2. Now, you ask me something. Ask me a question about the people in this picture.
_____   ____   ____

3. _(Point to the windows)_ Tell me what these are in a sentence.
_____   ____   ____

4. _(Point to the woman gardening)_ This is what I did last year. Tell me in a sentence what I did last year. _____   ____   ____

5. Tell me one thing you did yesterday in a sentence.
_____   ____   ____

I'm going to tell you some words from the picture. You tell me if they are the same or different. Do these words from the picture sound the same?

6. Grass/brass- are they the same or different? _____   ____   ____

7. Girl/curl- are they the same or different?   _____   ____   ____

8. Man/man- are they the same or different?   _____   ____   ____

End of Assessment

SCORING KEY

Beginning English Speaker (BES)
Intermediate English Speaker (IES)
Advanced English Speaker (AES)

BEGINNING LEVEL
1. student's name
2. student correctly says where they are from
3. student correctly says 1st letter of their name
4. student's age
5. 12
6. student obeys command correctly
7. student draws a road
8. a girl (or any correct female human noun)
9. It is a sun.
10. trees
11. They are playing (football or sports or a sport).
12. tired

INTERMEDIATE LEVEL
1. sun, clouds, or sky
2. 24
3. The boys (past tense verb or past continuous verb) yesterday.
4. I ate (a) _____ yesterday.
5. student spells first name correctly
6. student's birthday
7. my family/they + correct verb tense
8. student correctly pronounces sentence
9. student correctly pronounces sentence

ADVANCED LEVEL
1. student uses will/might/or future tense verb to make prediction about the picture
2. student asks you correctly worded question about picture
3. They/these are windows.
4. You gardened/planted last year.
5. student uses past tense correctly in sentence about self
6. different
7. different
8. same

www.bilinguallearner.com

VOCABULARY CARDS
Topics: Home, School, Nature, Personal Hygiene

These vocabulary cards are easy to make and a great warmup activity to teach new words or review old ones. In order to make the cards, get a stack of index cards and write each word on a separate card in bold, clear printing. Under the word, draw or paste a small picture of the object. Then spend 5-10 minutes each day showing students the cards and having them name the object- I like to work in a round robin style, allowing each student multiple cards to try and letting them hold any card they name correctly. At the end of the warmup, I usually let the student with the most cards pick a small prize. I also tell students that if I see they are quietly paying attention to others trying to pronounce their cards, I will award them an extra turn. Below are the words/pictures to put on each card, organized by topic:

School- desk, pen, pencil, crayons, stapler, paper, clock, scissors, tape, glue, book, map, trashcan, bathroom, markers, computer, bookshelf, cabinet, classroom, bus, box, letter, number

Home- table, chair, sofa, lamp, door, window, house, floor, bathtub, toilet, roof, bed, closet, fridge, stove, radio, television, stairs, wall, sink

Nature- dog, cat, tree, girl, boy, baby, man, woman, horse, cow, bird, plant, fish, pig, spider, bee, duck, flower, grass, sun, moon, cloud, star, sky

Personal Hygiene- brush, comb, soap, toothbrush, toothpaste, towel, tissue, toilet paper, glasses, razor, shower, bath, clothes, shoes, pants, shirt, socks, coat, shampoo

ALPHABET & NUMBER CARDS

These cards are notebook paper-sized and laminated with all the letters of the alphabet on one side and the numbers 1-20 on the other side. Each student gets a card each day during Circle Time and we practice pronouncing each square of the card with the following steps:

- Teacher shows students the number or letter to say. Students put their finger on it.
- Teacher says the number or letter/sound and students listen. Then, students repeat as a group.
- Individuals repeat the number or letter/sound (Round Robin style is fine).
- Repeat above steps with the next number/letter.

We do this each day at the beginning of the lesson for 10-20 minutes, saying all the letters/sounds of the alphabet and then turning the card over and repeating the steps above with the numbers in sets of 10. After students practice this activity for 4-8 lessons, try letting a student point out the letter or number on the card and make sure the other students put their finger on the correct letter/number and pronounce correctly. The student leader can ask others to re-pronounce, if necessary.

NUMBER CARD

1	2	3	4	5
6	7	8	9	10
11	12	13	14	15
16	17	18	19	20

ALPHABET CARD

Aa	Bb	Cc	Dd	Ee
Ff	Gg	Hh	Ii	Jj
Kk	Ll	Mm	Nn	Oo
Pp	Qq	Rr	Ss	Tt
Uu	Vv	Ww	Xx	Yy
Zz				

Dialogues

The following dialogues are a great way to facilitate a controlled practice of the concepts/vocabulary students have learned. Discuss and define any necessary vocabulary, verb conjugations, and/or grammar structures. Write the dialogue on chart paper and read through it with the students- first the teacher pronounces each line of the dialogue and then the students read/repeat it chorally. Also, brainstorm/write out some options for the blanks. After, have pairs practice for a few minutes and then have pairs act out their dialogue for the group.

For very young students, you might have a 2 line dialogue so students can practice by copying your model, rather than by reading. You might also have each student present the dialogue to the class with you as their partner since very young students may not be able to practice in unsupervised pairs.

Dialogue #1: To Be
Student A- Hello, what is your name?
Student B- My name is _____. What is your name?
Student A- I am _____. It is nice to meet you.
Student B- Nice to meet you, too. Goodbye.

Dialogue #2: Greetings
Student A- Hello, how are you?
Student B- I am _____. How are you?
Student A- I am _____. Thanks for asking.
Student B- Goodbye.

Dialogue #3: Can I?
Student A- Hello, can I use a pencil?
Student B- Yes, you can, because I have (#) pencils. Can I share your eraser?
Student A- You can share my eraser. Thank you.
Student B-You are welcome.

Dialogue #4: Demonstratives
Student A- Good morning. Do you know what this is?
Student B- Yes, this is a _____.
Student A- Thanks, that is helpful.
Student B- You are welcome. What are those?
Student A- Those are _____.
Student B- Thanks, goodbye.

Dialogue #5: Numbers/Birthday
Student A- Today is my birthday!
Student B- Wow, Happy Birthday! How old are you?
Student A- I am ____ years old. How old are you?
Student B- I am ____ years old. How old is your sister/brother?
Student A- She/he is ____ years old. Goodbye!
Student B- See you later!

www.bilinguallearner.com

 # Songs and Chants

Songs and chants are a great, fun way for students to practice the language concepts they have learned with no pressure. All of these can be sung by anyone, no matter how untrained the singer. Don't be self-conscious! Put all songs on chart paper for students to follow along as the teacher points to the words (for readers and non-readers alike). After students have learned a song, sing it with them every few days to practice, have fun, and review the concept during warmup or closing parts of the lesson. Also, after students get to know the song. try having one student point out the lyrics on chart paper and another student preform any song hand motions, while the rest of the class follows along.

"To Be" chant/handclap
* This chant is best sung to the beat of clapped hands/thighs in a rapid 1-2 rhythm:
I am *(1 hand clap)*
You are *(1 hand clap)*
He is, she is, it is. *(3 faster thighclaps- 1 for each conjugation)*
We are, *(1 hand clap)*
They are, *(1 hand clap)*
Present Tense To Be! (*3 faster thighclaps- 1 for each word*)

"Alphabet Song"
*It's lovely to play guitar along with this song, the chords are simple and listed below in caps. You can type the capital letters below into a search engine with the phrase guitar chords *and you'll find the correct chord fingering if you don't know chords.*
D-G-D, G-D-A-D
D-G, D-A (2x)
D-G-D, G-D-A-D
A, b, c, d, e, f, g,
H, i, j, k, l, m, n, o, p
Q, r, s,
T, u, v,
W, x, y, and z,
Now I know my a-b-c's
Next time won't you sing with me!

"This and That" chant
*This chant has a flowing1-2-3-4 rhythm.
These are the flowers
That house those bees
And that is the bird
That lives in this tree.

www.bilinguallearner.com

"This is the Way" song

*This song is sung to the tune of "Here We Go Round the Mulberry Bush" and is fun and easy to accompany with the guitar (repeating chords G, D7). You can type the above song title into a search engine with the phrase guitar chords and you'll find the correct chord fingering if you don't know chords. Students can do accompanying hand movements to show showering, brushing teeth, and combing hair while they sing.

This is the way we take a shower,

Take a shower,

Take a shower,

This is the way we take a shower when we wake up in the morning.

This is the way we brush our teeth,

Brush our teeth,

Brush our teeth,

This is the way we brush our teeth when we wake up in the morning.

This is the way we comb our hair,

Comb our hair,

Comb our hair,

This is the way we comb our hair when we wake up in the morning.

Short Stories

These little stories are a simple way to tie together all the concepts the students have been taught during the week's ESL lessons. First, discuss, define, or review any necessary vocabulary, verb conjugations, and/or grammar structures in the story. Write the story on chart paper and read it slowly to students, pantomiming all the parts of the story to help students understand. Then, read it again, pointing out each word as you read while students only listen. Read it a third time, inviting students to read along (even young children who can't read will eagerly try to "read" along with you, saying many incorrect words or babble- this is fine). Finally, have a student translate the story, so all can understand its meaning. Then have students answer the questions orally.

Story #1- "Friends at School"

Two friends at school are named Mary and Joe. They are both students. Mary is a girl. Joe is a boy. They ride the bus. They are both good students. I am the teacher of Mary and Joe☺.

1. Who is Mary?
2. Are Joe and Mary friends?
3. Where are Joe and Mary?
4. Who is the boy? Who is the teacher?

Story #2- "Friends at Home"

Mary and Joe ride the bus home. Can Mary do homework at Joe's house? Joe says yes. Can Joe use Mary's spelling book? Mary says that the spelling book is on the chair. She gets the book for Joe. They do spelling homework at the table. Mary spells her name with the letters M-A-R-Y and Joe spells his name with the letters J-O-E.

1. Joe and Mary ride the _____.
2. Can Joe use the book?
3. Where is the book?
4. Spell Mary's name.
5. Spell Joe's name.

Story #3- "Friends in the Garden"

Mary and Joe play in the garden. This is fun. Joe sees a bee in a tree. Mary sees that bee. Joe and Mary see a spider in a flower. This is a pretty flower. There are 10 trees in the yard and 20 bees in the trees.

1. Where do Joe and Mary play?
2. What do they see in the yard?
3. How many bees are in the trees?
4. Do Joe and Mary have fun?

Story #4- "Clean Friends"

Mary and Joe like to look good at school. Mary combs her hair before school. Joe brushes his teeth after breakfast. Today is Mary's birthday. Joe gives her a new comb. Joe says *Happy Birthday* to Mary. Mary is happy.

1. Who has a birthday today?
2. Who says *Happy Birthday*?
3. What does Joe give Mary?
4. Is Mary happy or mad?

ACTIVITIES

These activities can be developed and used as the main part of the lesson or simplified to be used in warmups and closing activities.

CIRCLE SPEAKING ACTIVITY

This is an oral repetition activity that goes well after the main part of the lesson has taken place. It's good to use some of the structures and vocabulary from the lesson in this activity. Be sure to define/explain any new vocabulary or concepts. Write one of the prompts below on the board with the corresponding choices/word bank for the blank part. Read the prompt and corresponding word bank aloud so all students can hear the correct pronunciation. Read them aloud again and have students repeat after you. Then have each student say the sentence with their own answer for the blank.

I've included 1 example of a prompt for each week- for the other days, you can create prompts based on your lessons.

You might shorten the prompts to 1 sentence for young children who can't read yet.

Week 1 Prompt:
This is a _____. There are five _____.
WORD BANK- desk/s, pen/s, pencil/s, crayon/s, paper/s, book/s

Week 2 Prompt:
Can you spell the word _____? It starts with the letter _____.
WORD BANK- table, chair, bed, sofa, lamp, door, window, house, t, c, b, s, l, d, w, h

Week 3 Prompt:
I like to draw pictures of _____. This is a picture of _____ trees.
WORD BANK- dogs, cats, flowers, fish, babies/ twelve, twenty, fifteen, eleven, seventeen

Week 4 Prompt:
This is the way I _____. That is the way I _____.
WORD BANK- brush my teeth, comb my hair, take a shower

SPELL YOUR NAME ACTIVITY

This activity is really fun for students to try once they've had some practice pronouncing the letters of alphabet. Put the two sentences below on the board or chart paper. Model how to do the activity by writing your name in the blank. Then read the 2 sentences and spell your name, pointing to each letter as you say it. Then have each student write their name on scrap paper and practice saying each letter with a partner. Finally, have each student come to the board, say the sentences with their name in the blank and then spell their name aloud for the class.

My name is _____.
This is how to spell my name.

OBSERVATION WALK ACTIVITY

In this activity, the teacher takes the students on a walk around the school grounds and points out objects whose names students are learning in their vocabulary lessons for that week. The teacher can chatter away in English during the walk, just letting students hear the authentic sound of the language. Then, every few minutes, the teacher should stop to point out, pronounce, and have students repeat the name of an object. After about every 5 objects, it's good to say/pantomime a sentence about that object, having students repeat it and try to understand the sentence. This is a fun and stimulating activity, its focus is mostly on the stimulation of letting students stretch their legs while applying English to their surroundings. For the last few minutes of the walk, you might ask students to try naming some of the objects they see in English.

LANGUAGE EXPERIENCE ACTIVITY (LEA)

Provide some sort of interesting topic/activity for the students to generate a discussion using the vocabulary of this volume and using present tense since that is the only structure that they have learned in this class. The teacher should generate the first two sentences by referencing structure and vocabulary examples that have been hung around the room on chart paper- it is important to model these 2 examples for the class. After the activity, initiate a discussion about the activity where all students contribute. Then, have the students dictate sentences about the activity in Round Robin style that the teacher writes on chart paper. The class reads the sentences aloud together and then individuals can read the sentences aloud or have pairs read the sentences to each other.

GAMES

Games are such a motivating and engaging way for students to practice their language skills in a no-pressure environment. Below are some of my favorite language games:

Numbers Bingo
Hand out blank bingo cards (Appendix M) and have students fill in the numbers 1-20 (they'll have to repeat a few) in any mixed-up order on their card. Students can use beans or pebbles to place on the bingo card. First, read out each letter/number (bingo letter and number in bingo column). Second, repeat the letter/number. Third, give students about 10 seconds to find letter/number on their bingo board. Finally, write the letter/number that was called out on the board or chart paper, so students can check their English and also check that they have placed a bean on the correct spot. The first student to get five beans placed in a row/column, calls out "BINGO", and wins a prize. After someone wins, have students clear their boards of beans and start again. Collect the bingo boards after the game to be handed out again for the next game.

Letters Bingo
Hand out blank bingo cards (Appendix M) and have students fill in 24 alphabet letters in any mixed-up order on their card. Students can use beans or pebbles to place on the bingo card. First, read out each letter pair (bingo letter and letter in bingo column). Second, repeat the letter pair. Third, give students about 10 seconds to find letter pair on their bingo board. Finally, write the letter pair that was called out on the board or chart paper, so students can check their English and also check that they have placed a bean on the correct spot. The first student to get five beans placed in a row/column, calls out "BINGO", and wins a prize. After someone wins, have students clear their boards of beans and start again. Collect the bingo boards after the game to be handed out again for the next game.

Simon Says
In this game, the leader (can be teacher or student) gives different commands to the class. Before the game, the teacher can write/review several basic commands relating to the week's lessons and point to them as she/he speaks to help students with comprehension during game. Also, repeat each command at least twice. At the start of the game, everyone should be standing. If the leader says "Simon says…" then the class can follow that command. But, if the leader only says the command (without saying "Simon says…" first), then the students should not follow the command-anyone who does, is out of the game and must sit down.

This and That
All students stand and the leader names school objects in the classroom, preceded by the word *this* for objects close to the group or *that* for objects far from the group. The student must point down (this) or point out (that) depending on whether the teacher says *this* or *that* to name the objects. Students who point incorrectly must sit down. The student left standing is the winner.

This/That/These/Those
Follow the same procedures as in the "This and That" game (above), but also use the words *these* and *those* to name groups of objects. The student left standing is the winner.

Name It!
Spread out all the vocabulary cards (Appendix C- with the words covered, sticky notes work great for this) face down with students sitting in a circle around the cards. Allow each student to choose a card and pronounce its name in English. If the student does this correctly, they can take off the post it and keep the card. The student with the most cards at the end of the game is the winner.

www.bilinguallearner.com

STRUCTURES

Structures are best used in the beginning stage of teaching a new English language concept because they provide clear cut rules that students can memorize and refer to in learning. Generally, it is best to teach the structure as the first or second lesson in the theme, maybe after a motivating game or song to introduce the topic. To teach these structures, write the rule and examples on chart paper. Then, discuss with class the rules above the structure chart. Read the statement/question with each pronoun while students listen for pronunciation. Then, read each again and students repeat. Call on a few individuals to pick a pronoun and read aloud each row of the structure. Then have each student read an example slowly in Round Robin fashion while another student points that example out on the corresponding row of the structures chart. For further written practice, have students write some statements/questions using each type of pronoun and a few named nouns to substitute for the pronouns; students can then share their sentences with the class.

1. CAN STRUCTURE

Rules- *Can* is used with a second verb to show what is or is not possible. All pronouns use *can* the same way.

- *Can* is followed by a second verb.
- For negatives, we add the negative word *not* between the two verbs.
- For questions, we place *can* at the beginning of the sentence.

	(Question Word)	Subject/Pronoun	+ Verb	(Negative)	+ 2nd Verb	+ Rest of sentence
+		I/we/you/they/he/she/it	can		run	to school.
-		I/we/you/they/he/she/it	can	not	run	to school.
?	Can	I/we/you/they/he/she/it			run	to school?

Examples:
Can Jim (he) have a snack? No, Jim cannot have a snack.
Can you and I (we) go to the park? No, you and I cannot go to the park.
Can you help me? Yes, I can help you.
Can Sue and Rosa (they) attend the show? Yes, Sue and Rosa can attend the show.

2. TO BE STRUCTURE

Rules- Use this structure to show a state of being, whether it is permanent or temporary.

- Three different forms of *to be* match the different pronouns/ 'persons'.
- For negatives, we add the negative word *not* after the *to be* verb.
- For questions, we place the *to be* verb at the beginning of the sentence.

	(Question Word)	Subject/Pronoun	+Verb/s	(Negative)	+ Rest of sentence
+		I	am		tired.
		He/she/it	is		a student.
		We/you/they	are		fast.
-		I	am	not	tired.
		He/she/it	is	not	a student.
		We/you/they	are	not	fast.
?	Am	I			tired?
	Is	he/she/it			a student?
	Are	we/you/they			fast?

Examples:
I am a boy.
Felipe (he) is angry.
Sam and I (we) are friends.
Jimmy and John (they) are brothers.

3. DEMONSTRATIVES STRUCTURE

Rule- Use *this/these* for close objects; use *that/those* for far objects.

CLOSE Object/s	+Verb	+ Rest of sentence
This	is	a pen
These	are	books

Rule-

FAR Object/s	+Verb	+ Rest of sentence
That	is	a pen
Those	are	books

Examples:
This is a bee.
That is a tree.
Those are sweaters.
These are kids.

www.bilinguallearner.com

4. PRESENT TENSE STRUCTURE

Rules- Use this structure when the action is general, when the action happens regularly or all the time, or when the statement is always true.

- For positive sentences, we do not use the helping verb.
- For negatives and questions, we add the helping verb *do (not)*.
- For he/she/it, we add *s* to the main verb or *es* to the helping verb.

	(Question Word)	Subject/Pronoun	(Negative)	+Verb/s	+ Rest of sentence
+		I/we/you/they		run	to school.
		He/she/it		runs	fast.
-		I/we/you/they	do not	run	to school.
		He/she/it	does not	run	fast.
?	Do	I/we/you/they		run	to school?
	Does	he/she/it		run	fast?

Examples-
I sleep in my bed.
It runs fast.
We do not run to school.
She does not run fast.
Do you run to school?
Does he run fast?
The ice (it) melts fast.
Does it melt fast?
It does not melt fast.
We run to school.
Sam and I (we) write slowly.
Do Sam and I write slowly?
Sam and I do not write slowly.
They run to school.
Jenny and John (they) talk a lot.
Do Jenny and John talk a lot?
Jenny and John do not talk a lot.
John does not talk a lot.

B	I	N	G	O
		FREE SPACE ☺		

NOW AVAILABLE!

ESL for Beginners Volume Two

Visit the website www.bilinguallearner.com to see our newest eguide, *ESL for Beginners Volume Two* where you can order it for just $7.95!

The book version of *ESL for Beginners Volume Two* is not available yet, but Like and Follow us on our Bilingual Learner Facebook and Twitter pages to see details about it very soon!

www.facebook.com/bilinguallearn
www.twitter.com/bilinguallearn

SALE!

All PDF versions of our guides are on sale now at www.bilinguallearner.com for just $7.95 and no shipping/handling costs necessary!

NEW PROMOTION!

Book versions of our guides come with a FREE CD and FREE domestic shipping/handling when you order them at www.bilinguallearner.com
You can also request an author-signed guide.

Printed in Great Britain
by Amazon.co.uk, Ltd.,
Marston Gate.